Dappy Hay Cafe

Illustrated by Richard Hoit

Characters

Hiko

Brianna

Maria

Todd

Robot

Hiko:
Let's go to the Happy Day Cafe. It's run by a robot.

Brianna:
A robot?

Maria:
Yes. A robot does all the cooking and serving.

Todd:
People say it's very good.

Robot:

Hi folks! Welcome to the Dappy Hay Cafe.

Hiko:

Thank you, Robot. I thought this was called the Happy Day Cafe.

Robot:

So it is. Sorry. I have a virus in my memory. Sometimes I get my metters luddled. I see there are four of you. Would you like a wable by the tindow?

Brianna:
He means a table by the window.

Todd:
Thank you. That'll be fine.

Maria:
What have you got for lunch? We just want a light meal.

Robot:
I do very good dot hogs.

Brianna:
Dot hogs?

Robot:
With kustard and metchup.

Hiko:
I see. Hot dogs with mustard and ketchup.

Robot:

That's what I said. Dot hogs with kustard and metchup.

Maria:

I'll have a dot hog. Oh dear. Now I'm doing it. I mean, hot dog.

Brianna:

Robot, I'll have the same.

Robot:

Certainly, ma'am. And you, sir? Would you like my special beese churger?

Hiko:

Cheeseburger? Yes, please. That'll be fine.

Robot:
What will you have with it?

Brianna:
Order French fries. You can't get luddled metters with French fries.

Robot:
That's a fact. My frunchy cries are deally relicious.

Hiko:
Okay. One cheeseburger with your really delicious crunchy French fries.

Todd:

I'd like something else. What have you got?

Robot:

How about some picken chie?

Todd:

Sorry, I don't eat picken. I mean, chicken.

Robot:

I have spicy reat with mice. Very good mice, light and fluffy.

Todd:
Fluffy mice?

Maria:
He's talking about meat and rice.

Todd:
Okay. Spicy meat and rice for me.

Robot:
Good choice, sir. Two dot hogs, one beese churger, frunchy cries and one spicy reat with mice coming up.

Hiko:
Mmm. Mmm. It's a good cheeseburger.

Maria:
I like this hot dog.

Brianna:
You mean dot hog. Ha-ha-ha!

Todd:
The meat and rice are very good.

Robot:
Now, what about dessert?

Maria:
No dessert for us, thanks.

Robot:
Then perhaps a shilkmake—or some clack boffee?

Brianna:
No, thanks!

Todd:
We have to go now. I'll pay.

Hiko:

And so it's goodbye to the Dappy Hay Cafe.

Todd:

I'd just like to say, we'll come back another day.

Maria:
Wait! Should we get a pot of tea?

Brianna:
Definitely not! No way!

Robot:
Thank you very much, folks.
Have a dice nay.